WILSON

READING
SYSTEM

STUDENT
READER
TEN

THIRD EDITION

by Barbara A. Wilson

Wilson Language Training
175 West Main Street
Millbury, Massachusetts 01527-1915
(508) 865-5699

ISBN 1-56778-076-8   Student Reader Ten   Item# SR10AB

THIRD EDITION (revised)

The Wilson Reading System is published by:

Wilson Language Training Corp.
175 West Main Street
Millbury, MA 01527-1915
United States of America   Tel#(508) 865-5699

Printed in the U.S.A.

STEP

10

Concepts

Adding Suffixes to Changing Basewords

10.1   - v-e exceptions: ice, ace, age, ate, ile, ite, ine

10.2   - Spelling Rule: Adding a suffix to a baseword ending in e
        (taping, lately)

10.3   - Spelling Rule: Adding a suffix to a one syllable closed or
        r - controlled baseword (starred, shopful)

10.4   - Spelling Rule: Adding a suffix to a multisyllabic baseword
        when the final consonant must double (regretting, controlled)

10.5   - Additional suffixes: ic, al, ible, ous, ist, ism, ity, ize, ary,
        ery, ory, ent, ence, ant, ance

service	Venice	Alice
terrace	palace	justice
notice	practice	office
menace	necklace	message
garbage	image	cottage
scrimmage	cabbage	hostage
manage	village	passage
damage	luggage	package
voyage	bandage	postage
advantage	language	shortage

10.1 A

climate	senate	separate
pirate	private	considerate
chocolate	delicate	opposite
definite	favorite	engine
medicine	examine	imagine

package	voyage	bandage
postage	advantage	justice
notice	practice	office
menace	delicate	opposite
definite	favorite	engine

malice	crevice	poultice
apprentice	novice	precipice
avarice	chalice	lattice
pumice	edifice	solace
Candace	linkage	savage
vintage	salvage	heritage
tutelage	cartilage	pillage
appendage	coinage	yardage
orphanage	pilgrimage	breakage
shrinkage	leakage	wattage

10.1 B

feminine	masculine	discipline
destine	famine	predestine
doctrine	jasmine	infinite
granite	respite	futile
fragile	fertile	docile

ate = /ĭt/

adequate	deliberate	literate
accurate	immaculate	palate
elaborate	illiterate	ultimate
articulate	inanimate	duplicate
triplicate	corporate	estimate

ate =/āte/

anticipate	vaccinate	operate
rejuvenate	elevate	dictate
speculate	donate	vacate
incorporate	pollinate	ventilate
calculate	demonstrate	equate

ate =/āte/,/ĭt/

advocate	separate	duplicate
articulate	triplicate	elaborate
deliberate	estimate	designate
alternate	aggregate	animate
inanimate	corporate	incorporate

1. Will you please take this message to Mrs. Flander's office?

2. Hopefully I don't have to eat this cabbage.

3. We're staying in the cottage on the beach with my uncle's family.

4. Did the package come from Venice?

5. The voyage on the sailboat was thrilling.

6. I need a bandage for this cut on my finger.

7. How did Camilla manage to misplace the bags of luggage?

8. There is a crowd in the small village for the road race.

9. My team has the advantage now.

10. Did the hurricane cause this damage to the terrace?

1. Chocolate milk with cookies is my favorite treat.

2. Alice and Sue rode on the donkey.

3. Fernando gave Carmen a necklace for her birthday.

4. Football practice was held despite the rain.

5. I visited Mom's office on Friday.

6. I think pirates raided that place long ago.

7. The clubhouse is fun because it is private and quiet.

8. I like to imagine everyone happy.

9. The doctor gave me medicine for the flu.

10. Did you notice the cockroach in the corner?

1. The hostage is not yet safe.

2. The passage leads to the old bowling alley.

3. The football player has a torn cartilage.

4. The postage for the package is much too costly.

5. The passage to the city was blocked by the destruction of the bridge.

6. There is a terrace and balcony outside the hotel room.

7. A trip to Venice is just a dream.

8. The rummage sale will be held "rain or shine."

9. We're trying to salvage any possible items from the horrible fire.

10. Joseph is a novice painter and sometimes he is not very careful.

1. Rosa has three children who have good discipline.

2. The detectives will examine the evidence carefully.

3. The elaborate plan was unsuccessful.

4. I hope to apprentice to the master carpenter in my town.

5. That boy seems destined to spoil our fun.

6. The fertile ground at the mouth of the river is good for growing rice.

7. Marvin sent a duplicate copy with his letter.

8. The kitchen looks immaculate!

9. Have you had some of this jasmine tea?

10. That granite wall is massive.

1. Dad is always considerate of Mom's feelings.

2. The package quickly came to our satisfaction.

3. It feels good to be so literate.

4. A disproportionate amount of taxes goes to that cause.

5. An orphanage was started by William Still for black children.

6. A bandage for his cut helped reduce the pain.

7. Todd effectively ran with the football for a yardage gain of ten.

8. We must avoid an energy shortage and conserve whenever possible.

9. Janet has passionate trust in the ability of man.

10. The company's corporate office is currently under renovation.

Football Scrimmage

Alice drank her chocolate milk and ran out the door. She was late for the Saturday football scrimmage. It was a fun game of touch football. Her best friend, Marjory, played on the opposite team.

Alice felt that her own team had a definite advantage, since Curtis was on her team. Curtis was a star on the high school football team. The scrimmage game was fun. Alice ran for a huge yardage gain. Then her team scored a touchdown. She was glad to be on the winning side.

computer	competed	amazing
latest	baker	tumbling
gracefully	likable	expensive
danced	imagining	announcement
noticed	privately	damaged
definitely	likely	regulated
bravest	cared	sprinkler
desirable	advancing	settlement
timed	struggling	safest
wisest	inspired	mistaken

cutest	hiding	broken
lately	safety	shining
hopeless	stared	bouncing
voter	widely	smoky
plateful	sizzler	ninety

sliding	spoken	shameful
simplest	handling	bravest
completely	inflatable	trampled
included	giggling	escaping
postponement	mumbling	polluting

recognized	dislikable	pavement
littlest	paving	tattled
drizzling	stapler	pleasing
illustrating	struggled	safely
convinced	living	demonstrated

livable	spicy	biker
plunged	saving	sliced
ruler	bravely	candles
nicely	arrangement	safety
drizzled	slider	smoking

revoked	postponing	deprived
quoting	conniver	profiled
blameless	inflatable	postponement
exiled	staging	disgraceful
inclined	decorating	starving
precisely	provider	rebatable
deleting	interfered	stampeded
mundanely	completing	blamed
palpitating	fabricated	phased
sanest	tumbler	inclined

igniter	probed	intervening
ornately	forsaken	salable
pulverized	provider	sniper
slimy	victimized	uselessly
backstroking	conspired	providable

spineless	enhancement	disposable
continuing	spiny	quotable
settler	declared	completely
actively	nervy	timeless
woeful	shiny	cared

advancement	engagement	blameful
concentrated	entirely	pridefully
lunging	enticing	contemplating
winced	hazy	excitable
blameless	spiteful	timely
engraver	discharging	provider
remotely	noiselessly	slimy
balanced	observable	boggled
trembled	priceless	entanglement
officer	squarely	revolving

entirely	enlargement	quotable
comparable	insider	involvement
shamelessly	excusable	relivable
involving	transcribed	shaving
expiring	separately	infinitely

ce, ge

peaceable	outrageous	traceable
replaceable	pronounceable	chargeable
rechargeable	changeable	advantageous
dodgeable	untraceable	exchangeable
courageous	irreplaceable	unenforceable

plafest	extonely	spily
rinsiding	broneless	braggled
brageful	sproting	zanest
bricety	blakable	clotable
plomy	sperving	crigglement

flumbler	flomeless	stomest
crobed	capricated	constobable
stroper	brocisely	stoeful
plarving	twiggler	replamely
blacy	deproving	miper

1. I like this drink that quenched my thirst.

2. Beth was craving a tall glass of milk.

3. Mom glazed the cupcakes with blueberry frosting.

4. Ed was hoping that he could get a second plateful of food.

5. Jake fell on the pavement and scraped his leg.

6. The tot wiggled and giggled when she was tickled.

7. I am hoping to have lunch now because I am starving.

8. Tony was fondly stroking his pet dog, Chainy.

9. Even with his broken leg, Tim was in a joking mood.

10. Much to my amazement, I got the best score.

1. I can not understand Peter's mumbling.

2. The littlest child is the last in the lunch line.

3. The teacher asked the student to get the staples on the counter.

4. The cows went through the broken fence and into the nearby woods.

5. The team struggled to get the last score.

6. Mrs. Lord demonstrated the solution to the difficult math problem.

7. The sky was filled with sparkling, shining stars.

8. James is bouncing the baby on his lap.

9. Get the sliced bread in the pantry and the jar of peanut butter on the table.

10. I am sick of this drizzling cold rain.

10.2 A

1. Bravely, Jack plunged into the icy pond.

2. Danny traded his five last baseball cards.

3. The voter decided his choice for president at last.

4. Illustrating that story will be fun.

5. Nancy fumbled the football after she had made a great catch.

6. The biker recognized the farm house at the end of the long road.

7. Barb and Ed escaped from the bitter cold.

8. The kids had fun going through the sprinkler on the hot summer day.

9. My uncle turned ninety on his birthday last June.

10. We can't put the broken candles on the cake.

1. The boss pointlessly formulated a new plan.

2. The shady plot of land was on a nameless street.

3. Tommy trudged through the slush and finally arrived home.

4. It is highly unlikely that Paula will get nominated for the position.

5. Bert sat in amazement as his sister performed a solo.

6. Barb wakefully tossed in bed as she contemplated her problem.

7. Mr. Jones inspired me to go hunting for ducks.

8. The inmates felt that it was unlikely that they could escape.

9. Dan's lateness will be harshly punished.

10. The people were pridefully decorating the town hall for the reopening celebration.

1. Jake concentrated his effort on the advancement of a cancer cure.

2. James and Dick debated any likeness between the two crimes.

3. Mr. Fernandez is dedicated to the completion of the project.

4. Gramps grumbled about the new construction.

5. Jane finally settled on an appointment time.

6. Mr. Spatch will be investigating the violent crime.

7. Harry was blamed for the theft, but he did not do it.

8. Ken absolutely refuses to deliver the paper.

9. The company will begin distributing its new product on Friday.

10. Dave completely dominated the debate held in Hopedale.

1. Ted was arrested for drunk driving and his license was revoked.

2. I was unjustly blamed for deleting that item from the newsletter.

3. Bob was mistaken about the postponement of the event.

4. That company is now competing with a large corporation.

5. The people are striving to make this city more livable.

6. Mr. Potter shamefully used the organization for his own personal gain.

7. The news will hopefully include the latest development in the peace settlement.

8. Kevin and Jo-Ann will be announcing their engagement soon!

9. It's entirely speculation at the present moment.

10. It is important that the people of this nation understand their imcomparable wealth.

10.2 B

1. The price of a single family home is outrageous!

2. The problem with the product is traceable to its original development.

3. I think that the teacher is irreplaceable.

4. Do you think that battery is rechargeable?

5. It was a courageous effort on the part of the firefighter.

6. Some of these difficult words are hardly pronounceable!

7. The officer did not think the law was enforceable.

8. If you make the item chargeable to credit cards, you will increase your number of sales.

9. Their peaceable offerings are commendable.

10. Hopefully, the new location will be more advantageous.

Rail Expansion

Phase I of the construction project for the new railroad station began on Tuesday. The project is expected to be completed next summer. The station will include a waiting room, ticket booth and a concession space. There will be a 395 car parking lot.

Handicapped commuters will have designated parking spaces next to a ramp. This will provide easy access to the trains.

Local residents have expressed the need for a commuter train. The town's people are thrilled about the desirable change. Many have been actively involved with the development of the railroad. Mr. Park, selectman, declared, "This advancement has been anticipated by the people of Hopedale. We can hardly wait for its completion."

Vermont for Peace

In 1983, 750,000 Americans paraded in New York City for the cause of nuclear disarmament. Over 3,000 of these peaceful demonstrators were from Vermont. Many held signs that announced their position for a nuclear arms freeze. Vermonters were again seeking a peaceful solution to a contemporary problem.

Vermont is a proud state. It is a state of beauty and simplicity. Generally, Vermonters have strong feelings for tradition. This is still evidenced by the political forum of a town meeting.

In 1983, in town meetings across the state of Vermont, 177 out of 195 towns voted for the nuclear arms freeze. When the Vermonters later filed past the crowd in New York, town meeting democracy was making its voice heard. Signs described the 177 out of 195 vote. This sparsely populated state had been a leader in the return of the peace movement.

Civil Rights Heroes

It takes many united people to create a new direction in this world. However, within each large group force, there are often many brave, inspiring individuals. On December 1, 1955, Rosa Parks, an African American in Montgomery, Alabama, demonstrated such courage. Rosa refused to give up her seat on a bus to a white man. This refusal resulted in her arrest. Her action united the entire African American community in Montgomery. Finally, after 381 days of bus boycott, the lawmakers were forced to end segregation on the city's transportation.

Martin Luther King, Jr. was an individual who, through bravery, demonstrated that one man can have great effect on change. His leadership gave people hope. In 1963 he spoke to a rally of more than 200,000. He outlined a plan for America that would allow all people to eat together, go to school together and vote together.

Today, the South in America is quite different than it was in 1955 and 1963. Through the brave actions of many individuals, progress has been made for a new life in America.

tipped	dropping	banker
gripped	yanked	gladly
ripped	tubful	flapped
jumping	floppy	lasted
duster	nutty	robber

grinning	swished	shutting
trotting	stubbed	hitting
fistful	flabby	grabbed
drummer	camped	stepping
flatly	dreamed	dripped

flatter	justly	spinner
mending	mobbed	trapped
mending	spitting	scrubbing
snipping	flunked	lapped
spelling	jotting	dotted

trusting	dripless	flatness
thinking	junky	sadly
blended	hotter	nippy
fleeting	scouting	rusting
setting	dipped	trashing

softer	rubbing	mopper
brushed	misty	shaggy
hopped	resting	risky
cupful	limping	shopping
cutter	chopping	basked

shrinking	reddish	thinly
napped	stamped	colder
petting	nodded	hemmed
belted	badly	joining
stashed	slushy	madly

beating	boiled	growing
saddest	slipped	dashed
sitting	farming	maddest
neatest	popped	jabbed
barked	punches	humming
thinnest	listed	shopper
quitting	runner	claps
gladly	plugged	lifting
twisted	bigger	stopping
dimly	sleepy	leaping

moping	tapping	mopping
taping	riding	robbed
ridding	robed	cuter
sitting	striped	cutter
siting	stripped	waging

hopped	gripping	wagging
hoped	griping	scrapping
scraping	tapped	stripping
moped	striping	taped
mopped	griped	gripped

whirred	slurred	barred
charred	spurred	sparring
parred	furry	blurry
scarred	marred	tarring
jarred	starring	stirred

fixed	waxes	axing
mixer	taxing	foxy
waxing	fixer	taxer
taxes	mixes	fixing
mixed	axed	waxed

10.3 A - B

banged	stronger	lagged
ringer	hogging	mugger
flagged	dragging	soggy
sagging	tugged	slinging
lugging	drugged	wagging
rigged	bagger	swinger
foggy	logged	bigger
bogged	nagging	buggy
legging	strongest	singing
longer	chugged	hugging

bumming	topper	gabber
pesty	fibbing	gapless
lobbed	stabber	venting
sinful	crabby	stunned
snobby	plotting	bidding
spoiled	strutting	ribbed
jobless	trashing	basked
summing	sinning	bonded
baggage	slippage	sprouting
sobbing	fastest	thumped

pinned	pined	gapped
gaped	sniper	snipper
canned	caned	baneful
ragged	banned	raged
coper	doting	copper

dotting	lobed	canning
dinning	dining	lobbed
caning	shining	sniping
shinning	snipping	mating
sloping	matting	slopping

blinning	flobber	glapped
glipped	flober	glaping
grobed	flobbable	pladder
grobbed	craner	frugging
stridder	shrapping	flager

fripping	stapper	brammed
strotable	staper	crobed
graged	cronny	staby
breggest	glittest	thoping
cluter	glitest	chitted

1. The muddy path is hidden behind the meadow.

2. Cathy stabbed me with her pencil by mistake.

3. We will be quizzed in history soon.

4. The men are splitting the logs faster than yesterday.

5. Audrey gladly stopped shopping and headed home.

6. The grease dripped all over the kitchen!

7. Howard keeps dropping the throw from the third baseman.

8. The kids ran through the house shutting the windows quickly.

9. Ben screamed in pain when he stubbed his toe.

10. Bert will be the drummer in the band for a wedding on Saturday.

1. I enjoy sitting on the porch swing in the morning.

2. Paul had very chapped lips due to the day in the sun.

3. Janice snipped the roses to deliver them to her friend.

4. Ted was unable to stop the dripping faucet.

5. Is the shaggy dog a likable pet?

6. Trevor hopped on the bus to get out of the nippy cold.

7. The oven setting is too low for the cake.

8. Cindy mixed the paint until she had the color that she desired.

9. Sandra waxed the runners of the sled.

10. The chopper landed on the foggy highway to make the rescue.

10.3 A

1. After he chugged the drink, Ben felt sick.

2. The tot was nagging his dad all afternoon.

3. Paula was dragging the heavy sled across the snow.

4. A spider skillfully webbed a home in the corner.

5. Lou carefully mopped up the mess on the kitchen floor.

6. Mr. Blake hopped onto a city bus to go shopping downtown.

7. Cathy spotted the best site for camping.

8. Stanley gladly snipped flowers from the blooming garden.

9. It was a nippy day, but we held the yard sale anyway.

10. Jane tugged on her mother's skirt to get her attention.

1. Bert tapped loudly on the apartment door.

2. The children were nagging to be taken to the amusement park.

3. Jonathan badly scraped his leg when he hopped on the train.

4. The kids gripped the side of the toboggan as it raced down the slope.

5. The stars were brightly shining when the reddish sky darkened.

6. Sitting still is difficult for an active tot.

7. The dog sitting on the porch is barking at the children.

8. Gladly, the shopping was done before dark.

9. The runner twisted his ankle in the race.

10. The farmer stopped his tractor to check the oil.

1. The neighbors are splitting the cost of the new porch.

2. The reporter is summing up the facts for his exclusive article.

3. Marco went spinning off the road on a foggy afternoon.

4. The shopper was hoping to get some canned corn.

5. Ken was bragging about his shiny new truck.

6. Jenna is quitting her bad smoking habit.

7. The skinny lady did not need a slimming diet.

8. You can start the car by popping the clutch.

9. Our team's standing has been slowly slipping further from the lead position.

10. The jobless man hoped to obtain employment soon.

1. The rubbing alcohol might help clean this cut.

2. Sadly, the child's fibbing habit is well established.

3. If our candidate is elected, taxes will not be raised.

4. Barb made a foxy maneuver to win the game of backgammon!

5. The time seemed to be slowly dragging.

6. The detective was on duty to hopefully reduce the mugging.

7. He strongly hoped to avoid more taxes if at all possible.

8. The mugger escaped quickly into the hectic streets.

9. Tom has been waxing his new truck since twelve o'clock!

10. Steven was jobless due to his company's recent layoff.

1. Ben has been crabby since his team's loss in the football tournament.

2. Mom went to console the sobbing child.

3. I would like to designate the spending of the taxes that I pay.

4. Barney, the beagle, ran to his master while rapidly wagging his tail.

5. Janice was drugged in order to extract a tooth.

6. Jefferson County has banned the sale of fireworks.

7. Since its founding, the organization has been active in setting the town's goals.

8. Steve constantly griped about the rising taxes.

9. The thug robbed the rich man robed in jewels.

10. Ed ribbed Kevin about his reputation as a charmer.

School Break in Florida

Jimmy hopped on a city bus. He crossed town to Andrew's apartment. The boys were seniors at Brown Vocational High School. Jimmy dropped in to see Andrew for an unexpected visit.

Jimmy's strongest wish was to go to Florida on the February vacation break. He hoped to convince his friend. They plotted out the details. Andrew would gladly help Jim get his old Mercury Cougar in better shape. Fixing the brakes would be the first requirement.

The weather would be so much hotter in Florida. Andrew nodded in agreement. He agreed that it was a good plan. Jimmy left grinning. If all went well, they would soon be driving south for the winter break.

10.3 B

Cancer Treatment

A new treatment for cancer of the liver may bring hope to afflicted people. In the past, liver cancer was nearly always fatal, stunning the families of the victims.

Tumor removal from the liver is difficult and risky. Now, the tumor can be "zapped" with an ultrasonic probe of sound waves. This greatly reduces the chances of infection or excessive bleeding.

With procedures such as these, man is stepping closer to positive developments in the defeat of cancer. Advancements today are setting the way for a hopeful and healthy tomorrow.

A Trendy Place on the River

Jane and Paul Mitchell were dressed up and ready to go to dine at the new, trendy spot on the river. When they arrived, it was mobbed! They decided to wait in the lounge for a table. They ordered juice drinks and made their way over to a corner of the crowded room.

Jane liked the modern decorating flair, but Paul did not admire the contemporary furnishings. He preferred a more traditional atmosphere. However, the food had been highly praised so he looked forward to a yummy meal. The wait was much longer than expected. Finally, their name was called after $1 1/2$ hours!

Jane and Paul were starving! They were seated, but no waiter appeared. Paul flagged someone down, and at last their order was taken. The waiter was not very helpful and seemed to be in a crabby mood.

At last, Paul and Jane were served. The meals were well-prepared. The food was excellent, but the service was questionable. Paul tipped the waiter even though he was upset by the lack of attention.

Paul and Jane did not think they would recommend this new place to others. The food was good, but the place was too crowded and too impersonal for the costly charge.

10.3 B

forgetting	recurring	preferment
preferred	consulted	disbarring
blundering	forgettable	subsisted
transmitting	forbidden	murderer
propeller	remembering	profitable

forgotten	beginner	equipment
committed	permitting	creditable
laborer	uncontrollable	differed
silvery	conquering	impelled
transmitted	befogged	numbering

admitting	forgotten	committed
permitting	inferred	outfitting
compelled	occurring	unforgettable
acquitted	preferred	befitting
excelled	occurred	referred

unforgettable	outfitted	propeller
omitting	impelled	deferred
transferring	forbidden	committed
beginning	outfitter	admitted
unfitting	forgetting	admittedly

10.4 B

preventable	slandering	soliciting
controllable	impelled	transporting
plunderer	allotment	contained
committed	acquitted	plasterer
discovering	regretful	contested
marketable	labored	plastered
disbarred	forgotten	admitted
loitering	supportive	excelled
equipped	concealed	beginner
forbidding	expecting	concurred

1. The nightmare has been recurring for several weeks.

2. That violent film should be forbidden in this house.

3. The propeller of the plane will soon need repair.

4. The faces on the homeless beggars are un-forgettable.

5. The deferred payment will assist me in meeting my monthly bills.

6. The network transmitted the television program across the world.

7. The teacher permitted the class to be dismissed at one o'clock.

8. Dad was compelled to get his children many gifts.

9. Carlos excelled in computer science.

10. The outfitter for the scout camp has been delayed.

10.4 B

1. The students were forbidden to leave the school grounds.

2. I think the event is unforgettable!

3. Weather permitting, the picnic will be held on Sunday.

4. That client was referred by our agency.

5. We credited your account with a twenty-dollar deposit.

6. Tom blundered when he omitted the important name on the program.

7. Jane preferred to go to the shopping mall.

8. The suspected murderer was held without bail.

9. Heather admitted that she was fond of Lou.

10. The company outfitted the campers with equipment.

1. Ginger has been laboring in the kitchen for several days!

2. The unforgettable home run gave the crowd something to cheer about.

3. The numbering of the pamphlets was such a mindless task.

4. The children were forbidden to use the weight room at the health club.

5. Sandra preferred to stay at home, but Henry wished to go dancing.

6. The silvery propeller will need repair this year.

7. James preferred to pay the consulting fee before making a final decision.

8. Lou deferred payment for his new couch until he could afford it.

9. Peter quietly admitted his error to his wife.

10. Larry was compelled to call his girlfriend again.

1. I think our division comes up with the most marketable prospects.

2. The defendant was recently acquitted of that crime.

3. The army unlawfully plundered the city after its defeat.

4. The boys were escorted away by the cops for transporting stolen goods.

5. The soliciting of goods is not allowed in his office.

6. The town is not equipped with snowplows since it is located in the South.

7. Jim has excelled in computer science due to his strong dedication.

8. The crowd was uncontrollable when the team secured the pennant.

9. It is regretable that the company will shut down next year.

10. The big event will be happening in the park near my house.

Cajun Americans

The Mississippi River splits into hundreds of waterways near its mouth to create a delta. The rich lands near the mouth of the river were settled long ago by a sizable French population. French colonists in Canada were expelled by their governor in 1755 because they refused to swear allegiance to the Crown. They traveled south, and many found their way to Louisiana. French people were already living in New Orleans.

In the beginning, the people from Canada spoke French as it was spoken in Canada. Soon, however, Spanish, English and Indian words and phrases entered into their language. These immigrants became known as Cajuns. The proud Cajuns have maintained many of their customs. Today, they live fruitfully within Louisiana, continuing many traditions from the past.

10.4 B

Compulsive Shopping

Elizabeth is a compulsive shopper, and she is not alone. For many, shopping is more than a fleeting temptation. People may use it to fill emotional voids. Unlimited spending may take place with a credit card in hand.

Stores are constantly clamoring for a share of one's paycheck. Continually charging items can only add up to disaster.

The first step to recovery from compulsive shopping is to recognize that it can be an addiction. Carefully assessing one's finances is very important and budgeting is a requirement.

Ozone - The Earth's Protection

A sudden, sharp depletion of ozone in the upper atmosphere may be destroying the earth's protective layer. This may have severe consequences. Scientists are not prepared to say what exactly is causing the phenomenon. Pollution and changes in weather circulation are suspected.

To some experts, a major contributing culprit is a class of chemicals called chlorofluorocarbons. The U.S. banned the use of these as aerosol propellants in 1978. However, around the rest of the globe, use of these chemicals has been growing. The use of these compounds must be controlled. As man is discovering his past errors, he must quickly react to prevent further destruction.

10.4 B

Sugar Temptation

The Food and Drug Administration recognizes sugar as generally safe. There is no regulation of the amounts used by food companies. As a result, some foods contain an unreasonable amount. There are no laws forbidding this.

The responsibility, then, falls on the individual. People should be committed to the intake of a limited amount of sugar. Too much is unhealthy, as well as fattening! There are 4 calories per gram of sugar. Concentrated sweets can contribute indirectly to the storage of fat. The body releases insulin in order to process the sugar. Insulin then promotes additions to existing fat deposits.

It is not healthy to displace nutritional calories with empty sugar calories. Remembering this fact is admittedly difficult when faced with delectable treats! On the other hand, it is possible to reduce one's daily consumption by attending to the contents of any store-bought product. In this way, people can somewhat painlessly obtain a controllable allotment of sugar.

ent	ence	ous
al	ible	ary
ity	ism	ant
ance	ery	ory
ize	ist	ic

ery	ize	ic
ance	ist	ant
ory	ism	ible
ary	al	ous
ent	ence	ity

democratic	organic	graphic
alphabetic	acrobatic	alcoholic
classic	diplomatic	poetic
automatic	magnetic	demonic
microscopic	Arabic	cubic

accidental	arrival	professional
comical	festival	intentional
optional	sectional	nautical
original	fanatical	astrological
institutional	ornamental	sensational

irresistible	destructible	digestible
producible	irresponsible	reducible
sensible	resistible	convertible
forcible	invincible	responsible
collapsible	accessible	corruptible

dangerous	marvelous	famous
cancerous	joyous	continuous
murderous	thunderous	ponderous
carbonous	prosperous	pompous
hazardous	treasonous	rigorous

10.5 B

activist	motorist	romanticist
novelist	communist	absolutist
extremist	purist	organist
isolationist	pharmacist	fundamentalist
feminist	loyalist	nutritionist

absenteeism	communism	romanticism
organism	absolutism	criticism
extremism	mysticism	fundamentalism
magnetism	collectivism	cynicism
alcoholism	occultism	fanaticism

realize	purity	density
vaporize	sparsity	alphabetize
authenticity	equalize	revolutionize
immensity	rarity	tranquilize
victimize	magnetize	minority

ary, ery, ory

dictionary	bindery	supplementary
documentary	accessory	shrubbery
slavery	trickery	commentary
migratory	boundary	summary
refinery	crockery	sensory

existent	despondent	consistent
adherence	conference	persistent
occurrence	different	insistence
inference	respondent	coherent
indulgence	existence	correspondence

acquaintance	resistance	descendant
inhabitant	accountant	ignorance
performance	acceptance	attendance
accordance	inheritance	admittance
defendant	assistance	attendant

contradictory	desirous	functionary
arsonist	irresistible	modernize
governmental	expansionism	visionary
legendary	ignorant	classic
appearance	insistent	nervous
rancorous	indulgence	stationery
betrayal	annoyance	cannery
urgent	stationary	triumphant
bribery	missionary	collectible
absurdity	artistic	nutritionist

artistic	idealistic	originally
brutally	classicism	professionalism
accidentally	communalism	realistic
forcibly	capitalistic	emotionalize
fatalistic	alphabetical	functionally

discernibly	acrobatically	magnetically
capitalistic	realistically	automatically
accessibly	electronically	classically
intentionally	idealistically	alphabetically
authorizing	diplomatically	demonically

1. James has such a poetic style of writing!

2. The democratic system will be used to elect a new club president.

3. Bert has a very diplomatic way of making his feelings public.

4. James had an accidental fall on the steep incline.

5. The hotel will offer an optional, extended vacation plan.

6. M.J. and Dennis plan to bring their boys to the big spring festival in Portland.

7. The original painting was auctioned for two thousand dollars.

8. Tyrell has a rational mind yet I do not understand this report!

9. Kareen would like to become a professional boxer, but it is unlikely.

10. Jan is hoping to get a sectional couch for the living room.

1. The hurricane evacuation plan is very sensible.

2. Sherry was very strong and incorruptible.

3. My convertible car is so much fun to drive.

4. That ball team has dominated the games and seems invincible.

5. When Ed pours on his charm, he is irresistible!

6. It is important to establish sensible rules in the schools.

7. Alice gave a convincing argument, but Jane was not corruptible.

8. The teacher attempted to find out who was responsible for the classroom mess.

9. Those seats are not accessible to the general public.

10. The tent is collapsible and fits into this small pouch.

1. The thunderous applause at the end of Act I demonstrated the crowd's praise.

2. The pompous king came to power in the late eighteenth century.

3. The prosperous state is a good example of the man's policy.

4. The actor became famous after his most recent film.

5. Americans must regulate the disposal of hazardous waste.

6. The joyous occasion will be celebrated on November tenth.

7. I think Fred has been a marvelous addition to the staff.

8. The continuous music in the park has been quite pleasant!

9. The rigorous exercise has exhausted me.

10. Jim felt murderous when he was told the bad news.

10.5 B

1. Paula's absenteeism is not a very sensible way to pass.

2. Alcoholism is on the rise in our country today.

3. My idealism remains even though I have seen many negative things.

4. Look into the microscope and see the many organisms on the slide.

5. During the Revolutionary War, that family's ancestors were loyalists.

6. Janet would like to be a novelist, and she has the talent to succeed.

7. The activist is organizing a protest march for the cause.

8. The Communist Party lost votes in the last election.

9. I was dismayed to hear the negative criticism from the new prime minister.

10. Peg is a nutritionist who shares current information freely.

1. We'll hopefully revolutionize that company's inventory organization.

2. We must not allow the greedy people to victimize the helpless.

3. Most of the Arabic community is located on the west side of the city.

4. The sparsity of trees in this location indicates that we are near the top.

5. The extremists are in the minority.

6. Hopefully, this invention will revolutionize the industry.

7. It is amazing to see the scarcity of homes on this island.

8. If we magnetize these letters, we can demonstrate concepts to the class.

9. The immensity of the Gulf of Mexico is hard to imagine!

10. The spotting of an owl is a rarity.

1. The supplementary program will be offered next fall.

2. The cops stopped the chase at the city's boundary.

3. Trickery is rampant on Halloween.

4. The teacher wants a summary paragraph submitted by Friday.

5. The commentary on the debate was more interesting than the debate itself!

6. It is impossible to comprehend the position favoring slavery.

7. The migratory birds will soon be heading south.

8. The shrubbery along the side of the house needs trimming.

9. I felt a sensory overload with so much happening all together.

10. Dennis will get M.J. that accessory for her wardrobe.

1. We can't wait to attend the conference in November.

2. There's hundreds of different kinds of fish in this huge tank.

3. The entire family plans to go to the opening performance.

4. I hope we can find a good accountant to sort out this mess.

5. The poor and homeless in this nation need our assistance.

6. She was quite indulgent to let him eat that dessert!

7. You've established the fact that the policy was nonexistent at the time.

8. The president of the class made an inspirational acceptance speech.

9. I think that statement showed how ignorant the speaker is.

10. The defendant was insistent about his innocence.

10.5 B

1. When Cathy and Bert had their baby, it was a joyous occasion.

2. Maureen drives through town in the red convertible that was refurbished by her husband.

3. This institutional food is really not bad at all.

4. Tonight there is a television documentary on civil rights.

5. Speeding down the highway is quite dangerous.

6. Sid accidentally dropped his glass of wine on the carpet.

7. My uncle likes to describe the legendary event.

8. The army demands a rigorous training effort.

9. Jim's annoyance with the clerk was very evident.

10. I wish that humorous conversation was recorded.

1. Trevor has a very magnetic personality.

2. Classical music sounds marvelous at a live concert.

3. Consistency is so important when raising children.

4. Realistically, the program can't possibly be completed by its deadline.

5. Kevin intentionally walked the base runner.

6. Jane is emotionally involved with the homeless child.

7. Peg and Jim artistically decorated their new apartment.

8. Dennis was originally going to Detroit, but he was able to cancel the trip.

9. That puppy is irresistibly cute!

10. Cara accidentally spilled coffee on the living room rug.

10.5 B

Accomplishment

People often think others who meet with success must have more brains and luck than themselves. This is usually not true. What they may have instead is more self-discipline and the ability to make choices.

Success starts with choices. A person decides to pursue something. At this point, it must be realized that in selecting one goal, other goals must be left behind. For example, if a person states as a goal the completion of a woodworking project by a particular date, he or she is also choosing to give up other things. Saturdays must be spent on the project instead of visiting friends or doing errands. There is just not enough time to pursue all endeavors at once!

A feeling of anxiety must be overcome to make most choices that will move a person toward self-development. A person may wish to do the wood project but feel that he or she can't do it properly. This emotion can be expected whenever a choice is made to do something new and different.

Kierkegaard, a Danish philosopher, said that anxiety always arises when a person confronts the possibility of self-development. It is important to recognize this. If a goal is not chosen because of anxiety, a person will often feel depressed. Anxiety is normal and should be expected with each new goal.

(continued)

10.5 B

Accomplishment (continued)

Perseverance is the next challenge! Gratification is not instant. A person may say, "I just can't get motivated to start!" Motivation does not happen automatically– the wood might sit in a pile. A feeling of gratification will not occur for sometime. Motivation often does not "kick-in" until the end is in sight. At that point, when a person can start to feel a sense of satisfaction, he becomes highly motivated. That means that a project often must be started without motivation! Persistence must occur to drive a project continuously, often slowly, forward.

Success is not accidental. When people make a choice for self-development, despite the nervousness it produces, they have begun. In making the choice, other things must be relinquished. The first labors toward the goal must be started almost without motivation. As persistent action continues, motivation develops, and a goal will be met. The sense of accomplishment is grand, and a person then gains a step in the fulfillment of self-potential.

National Parks

America is beautiful. There are thousands of sensational sights across the nation. Many of these are preserved within the boundary of a national park. The wilderness is under governmental protection in geographical locations throughout the U.S.A. The national park system also manages valued historical monuments, famous battlegrounds, and scenic trails.

The national parks, for the most part, have been lovingly maintained. Seasonal attractions lure people for recreation and enjoyment. Those visiting the parks realize their responsibility to respect their beauty. However, 300 million people per year flood into the system. Conservation of the land, with all its glory, is a must. The national park system is a generous gift to every U.S. citizen. The people, in turn, must show thanks with a strong dedication to keep these parks in their original form.

Post Test Step Ten

A

necklace	likable	notice
lugged	arrangement	polluting
simplest	stubbed	mopping
privately	cupful	spinner
shaggy	moping	convinced

B

deliberately	trotting	mugger
continuous	enhancement	orphanage
irreplaceable	acquitted	climates
interference	immensity	recurring
responsible	enforceable	observable

Post Test Step Ten
!@#$%

deproving   cronny   striggler

clozable   explonely   glabbage

chogglement   tridest   torbiddest

flobbable   apmitting   blacy

frugger   prederring   deparred

---

1. Find and mark v-e exceptions: cott $\underset{v\times e}{\overset{ij}{\underline{age}}}$ en $\underset{v\times e}{\overset{\smile}{gi}ne}$

Cirlcle suffixes.

2. Make a chart like the one below using all words with suffixes.

Word	Baseword	Suffix $\underline{\overset{v}{}}$	$\underline{\overset{c}{}}$	Choose one:	dropped e doubled consonant just added suffix
e.g. giggling	giggle	ing			dropped e
pavement	pave		ment		just added suffix
capped	cap	ed			doubled consonant